Enid Blyton's
A SHOCK for SHEILA
AND OTHER STORIES

PRINTED IN GREAT BRITAIN
DEAN & SON Ltd.
41/43 Ludgate Hill LONDON EC4

This edition published by DEAN & SON, LTD. 1976

03 06508 2

A Shock for Sheila

SHEILA was spoilt at home. She was the only girl, and so her Mummy and Daddy thought she was wonderful. If Sheila had had a brother or sister, her parents wouldn't have thought she was quite so wonderful! She was really quite an ordinary little girl, not so nice as she might have been, because such a fuss was made of her.

Sheila didn't do anything for herself. Her Mummy did it for her. She hung up Sheila's clothes, she brushed her hair, she cleaned her shoes for her, she tidied her drawers, and she even picked up the things that Sheila dropped. Did you ever hear of such spoilings?

When Sheila came in from school she took off her hat and coat, of course —and just dropped them on the floor! She didn't dream of hanging them up. Oh no—Mummy could pick them up and do that. And Mummy did!

It wasn't till Sheila was sent to stay with Granny, that she discovered what a lot of things Mummy did for her—because Granny didn't do any of them, and so Sheila had to!

She had to clean her own shoes, for one thing. "And that won't hurt you!" said Granny, giving Sheila a pot of shoe-cream, a little brush, a bit of rag, and a duster. "Just see what a fine polish you can get on those shoes of yours."

"But I've never cleaned shoes before," said Sheila.

"Poor child! What a shame!" was all that Granny said.

Sheila soon learnt to polish her shoes nicely, to brush her own hair, and even to tidy her chest-of-drawers. But there was one thing she would *not* learn—and that was to hang up her clothes when she took them off!

No—as soon as she came in from school she did as she was used to doing—took off her hat and coat, and let them drop to the floor!

Granny didn't pick them up. Nobody picked them up. There they lay till Sheila wanted to put them on again. Granny was disgusted. She could *not* seem to make Sheila remember not to do that.

"How your mother has spoilt you!" she said to Sheila. "I didn't spoil your mother when she was *my* little girl—but then I had six children to see to, so there wasn't time to spoil any of them, not even the baby."

One day Sheila's mother sent her a parcel. In it were some new clothes she had made for Sheila. The little girl was simply delighted. There was a winter coat in red, with a red velvet collar and cuffs, and red buttons. There was a dear little round red hat to go with the coat, with a red velvet band on it, made into a bow at one side. There was a striped scarf and a pair of red gloves.

"Well!" said Granny, looking at them all. "Your mother is very, very clever, Sheila—just look at all these things she has made for you! She has even knitted a scarf and gloves to match. How kind of her! You will look very nice indeed!"

"Oh, Granny, can I wear them this afternoon?" cried Sheila, in delight. She thought she would look lovely in her new things—and, indeed, she did, for they suited her dark hair very well indeed.

"Now do take care of them, darling," said Granny. "They really are beautifully made. DON'T throw them on the floor when you come in."

"No, I won't," said Sheila. And she actually remembered not to that afternoon. She took them off carefully and hung them in her cupboard. Granny felt pleased.

But when Sheila had worn her new clothes a few times, she grew careless again—and two days later, when she came in from school, she flung them off, and down to the floor they all went as usual! Granny wasn't there, or she would have been cross. As it was, Sheila's new things just lay on the floor till she picked them up to put them on again in the afternoon.

The next day Granny told her that Mrs. Lacy from the farm was coming to tea.

"Will she bring that darling little puppy with her?" asked Sheila, who loved all puppies and kittens. "Oh, do tell her to, Granny—then I can play with the puppy while you are talking to Mrs. Lacy."

"Very well," said Granny. "I'll tell her she can bring the puppy."

Sheila raced home from school that afternoon to see the puppy. It was sweet. One side of its head was brown and the other was white, and it had a white tail that it wagged without stopping. Its name was Bunter, and it was the naughtiest little thing you can imagine!

Sheila rushed into the hall. She flung off her coat, hat, her scarf and gloves—and down to the floor they all went as usual! Then she went to shake hands with Mrs. Lacy—and to see the puppy!

"I'm so glad you've come, Sheila," said Mrs. Lacy, shaking hands with her. "This puppy is so naughty. He has chewed the end of your Granny's rug, and tried to eat Grandma's slipper! Do take him away and play with him."

So Sheila took the puppy to her bedroom, and they had a wonderful game.

"Bunter! I'll hide and you can find me!" said Sheila. So she hid behind the bed—and Bunter came running underneath on his four fat paws, his tail wagging like grass in the wind!

Sheila played with him till the bell went for tea. Then she picked Bunter up and took him downstairs. Granny gave him a saucer of milk and told

Sheila to sit down at the table. There was a lovely tea. Sheila forgot all about the puppy for a while, as she ate potted-meat sandwiches, and bread-and-butter, and honey, and chocolate biscuits.

"Where's that puppy?" said Mrs. Lacy, looking round for him. "He's finished his milk."

"Oh, he's probably asleep somewhere after his games with Sheila," said Granny. So nobody went to look for him till after tea. And do you know what he was doing all that time?

He had run into the hall, and had found all Sheila's clothes on the floor, where she had left them. Ah! What lots of things to chew!

Puppies simply love chewing things—and Bunter was a wonderful chewer. Mrs. Lacy said she felt sure he could chew up a dustbin, lid and all, if he really tried hard. Anyway, he was simply delighted to find a coat, a hat, two gloves, and a scarf to chew up!

He set to work. He chewed up the gloves so that they looked like rags. He chewed four big holes all down the scarf, and nearly made himself sick trying to swallow it. He chewed the velvet ribbon off the hat, and bit a hole out of the middle of it. That was fine! He thought he had managed the hat very well.

Then he began on the coat. That was a big thing to chew—but Bunter felt sure he could manage it. He loved the buttons. He worried at them till they were all off. He chewed the velvet collar and cuffs. He bit three holes at the back of the coat and two at the front. He really had a lovely time!

He was just pulling at the lining when he heard Sheila calling him.

"Bunter, Bunter, where are you? We've finished tea!"

"Woof!" said Bunter in a very doggy voice. He felt grand because he had had such a good chew.

"Where are you, Bunter?" called Sheila, and she came into the hall to find him. "Oh, Bunter, what are you doing to my clothes?"

"Woof, woof!" said Bunter proudly, and he sat up with a glove in his mouth as if to say "Look at the wonderful thing I have done!"

And then Sheila saw everything. She saw her ragged gloves—her chewed scarf—her spoilt little hat—and her beautiful coat quite, quite spoilt too, with all the buttons off and the collar and cuffs bitten to pieces.

"Oh, you *wicked* puppy!" she cried, and she burst into tears. "You bad, wicked creature! I'll whip you! Oh, Granny, Granny, come quickly! Something dreadful has happened."

Granny and Mrs. Lacy came running out in alarm. Whatever was the matter? When Granny saw the clothes lying on the floor all spoilt, she didn't know what to say. Mrs. Lacy was full of horror.

"Bunter shall be whipped!" she said. "Oh, the bad little thing—however did he manage to get all those things? Surely he didn't pull them down from the hall-pegs?"

"No," said Granny in a funny sort of voice. "No—I hardly think he did, Mrs. Lacy. I have an idea that Bunter is not so much to blame as Sheila. Sheila, did you throw all your clothes on the floor again this afternoon?"

"Yes," said Sheila, and she wept loudly. "But Bunter has no right to chew them up."

"You know that puppies chew everything they find on the floor," said Granny. "You knew that Bunter was here when you came home. And yet you carelessly threw your things down, all the same. You deserve to have them spoilt. I have no sympathy with you at all, Sheila. I will not have Bunter smacked. You are the one that should be smacked for causing your lovely new clothes to be spoilt. Now, if you want to make a noise like that, go upstairs and shut yourself into your bedroom where nobody can hear you. Then you can howl as much as you like!"

Sheila went upstairs crying bitterly. She sat down on the bed. Horrid Bunter! Horrid puppy!

And yet he didn't know that he was chewing up such nice things. He was only a puppy. Sheila knew that it was really all her own fault. After a while she dried her eyes and went downstairs. Mrs. Lacy had gone. Granny was sewing.

"Don't look crossly at me, please, Granny," said Sheila. "I know it was all my fault. I still like Bunter, though he spoilt my things. I'll write and tell Mummy—and I'll tell her it was through my untidiness. I'll never, never throw my things on the floor again."

"Good girl," said Granny, smiling over the tops of her glasses. "Well—you've still got your old things, luckily, so you've something to wear—and if the loss of your new clothes teaches you to look after your things in future, maybe it will be worth while!"

I don't think Sheila's Mummy will know her when she goes back! She does everything for herself now, and looks after her belongings as carefully as you look after yours. I hope her mother won't spoil her all over again, don't you?

Who Came Creeping in the Door?

OLD Man Hobble lived in a tiny cottage all by himself. He was very fond of ginger biscuits and big round peppermints, and he kept a tin of each on his mantelpiece.

He made the biscuits every Tuesday and the peppermints every Saturday, and when his old aunt came to see him on Wednesday and Sunday there were always plenty to offer her.

And then one day Old Man Hobble was puzzled. It was Wednesday and his aunt came to see him. He took the tin down from his mantlepiece and opened it. His Aunt looked inside.

"Dear me, Hobble," she said. "You've only got two biscuits left! Didn't you bake them yesterday as usual?"

"Yes, I certainly did," said Hobble. "I made a whole tinful. What a peculiar thing!"

And then on Sunday when his aunt came, and he took down his peppermint tin, what a surprise! There were hardly any peppermints there, although he had nearly filled the tin on Saturday.

"Somebody comes creeping in at your door when you go out shopping," said his aunt. "Yes, somebody comes in and takes your ginger biscuits and your peppermints, Hobble, no doubt about that!"

"Oh, dear!" said Hobble. "How very horrid! Who can it be? The children all come by my cottage on their way to and from school. I suppose it must be one of them. But the little thief will never own up."

"Of course he won't," said his aunt. "You must find out yourself."

"But how?" asked Hobble.

"I'll tell you," said his aunt, and she whispered into his ear. He nodded his head.

"Yes, yes, I'll do that! A very good idea of yours, Aunt. I'd rather not do the spying myself. I'll set all those things to do the work for me instead."

Well, the next day, before he went out shopping, Old Man Hobble set a few things about the room. He took a pin-cushion and in it he put six needles with big eyes. He went out and picked six stalks of corn and put them in a vase on his mantelpiece. Their ears rustled together prettily.

And then he put three pairs of shoes on the floor below the mantelpiece, with their six tongues sticking out well.

"There!" said Hobble. "Now do your work, all of you!"

He went out to do his shopping.

There were no biscuits or sweets taken from the tin that day, nor the next. But on the next day the tins were almost empty.

"Who is it that comes creeping through my door?" wondered Hobble. "It must be one of the children. What a pity!"

Now, the next day Hobble asked all the schoolchildren to come and see him. "I want to show you a bit of magic," he told them. "So come along."

The children were pleased. They thought Old Man Hobble was a very good conjurer, and they came crowding in after school.

"Now, children," said Hobble, "I want to ask you something. Someone has been creeping in at my door and has been taking my ginger biscuits and my peppermints. I don't know who it is. Before I find out by magic, I want to ask you if you know who it is? Will the silly little thief please be brave and own up? Then I will forgive him and he shall promise me never to do such a bad thing again."

But nobody owned up. The top boy of the class, Billy Bold, spoke quite rudely to Old Man Hobble.

"Who wants your old biscuits and sweets? We get enough money to buy all we want!"

He was a big boy, strong and handsome. He was a clever boy, too, and all the children looked up to him.

"Yes," they said, anxious to say the same as the great Billy Bold. "Yes, we get enough money of our own to buy biscuits and sweets without bothering about *yours*, Old Man Hobble!"

Hobble looked rather sad. "Well, I shall have to do a bit of magic, then, to find out what I want to know," he said. "Now, listen, children. I have done no spying myself, but others have watched for me. See, these are the watchers!"

He pointed to the pin-cushion with the six needles, to the six stalks of corn in their vase, and to the three pairs of shoes below. The children stared in wonder, and Billy Bold and one or two others laughed scornfully.

"He's mad," said one of them, behind his hand. Old Man Hobble heard.

"No," he said, "I'm not mad. You will soon see how clever I am, not mad!"

He threaded the six needles with white thread and then stuck them into a piece of black cloth.

"Whom did you see with your six little eyes?" said Old Man Hobble in

a loud voice to the needles. "Tell me his name, needles!"

And before the children's astonished eyes the six needles began to sew all by themselves. Stitch after stitch they made in the black cloth, and the white threads showed up clearly.

"Billy Bold!" they wrote in big white stitches. "Billy Bold!"

"Billy Bold!" said all the children in low, shocked voices. "Is he the thief?"

"It's rubbish," said Billy Bold, loudly. "All a silly trick. How dare you, Old Man Hobble?"

The six needles had now used up all their thread, and they stopped sewing. Old Man Hobble took down the vase of corn-stalks. Their dry ears rattled together. He set them on the table near the children, and bent over them.

"Whom did you hear, with your

six ears, golden corn?" asked Old Man Hobble. "Whisper me his name!"

Then, as if they were blown by the breeze, the six ears of corn began rustling together and whispering. "It was-s-s-s Billy Bold! It was-s-s-ssss Billy Bold! Ss-ss-ss!"

The children could hear what the corn whispered quite plainly. They looked scared. Billy Bold went rather pale. But he was still very defiant.

"Pooh! Another trick! What nonsense!"

"And now we will see what my shoes say," said Old Man Hobble. "They have tongues to speak with. Shoes, who comes creeping in at my door when I am gone?"

All the six tongues flapped and spoke at once. "Billy Bold! Billy Bold! Billy Bold!"

Then Billy Bold sank down suddenly into a chair, his face very white. "It's queer," he said. "It must be magic after all. I don't understand it."

All the children looked at him. "*Was* it you, Billy Bold, who took the biscuits and the sweets?" asked a boy.

"It was, it was, it was!" shouted all the shoe-tongues, and the ears of corn whispered again.

Billy Bold hung his head. "Yes, I took them," he said. "I'm so ashamed. Now you all know me for what I am! Old Man Hobble, I'm sorry."

"Are you?" said Old Man Hobble, in a mild sort of voice. "Well, people who are sorry for doing wrong usually do something to show they are."

"Yes, they do," said the children. "Billy, what are you going to do?"

"I don't know. But I'll do *something*," said Billy, his face now a bright red. "Please, all of you, don't tell my mother. She'd be so upset."

"We won't tell anybody, if you really *are* sorry," said Old Man Hobble. "It shall be a secret."

Well, Billy Bold kept his word and tried to show that he really was sorry. He came and weeded Old Man Hobble's garden for him. He cleaned out his hen house twice a week. And he mended his gate for him so that it would open and shut properly.

Sometimes Old Man Hobble offers him a biscuit or a sweet, but Billy always shakes his head. "I can't bear the taste of ginger or peppermint now," he says. "Thank you all the same, sir!"

It was a queer way to find the name of the thief who came creeping in at the door, wasn't it? I'd like to have heard those shoe-tongues shouting. It *would* have given me a surprise!

The Strange Bicycle

1. John and Jane watched the circus vans go by—how gay they looked as they went down the lane! "Galliano's Circus" was painted on each caravan and cage.

2. Now when the two children went up the lane on their way home, John suddenly saw something lying in a muddy ditch. "Whatever is it?" he said. "It can't be a bicycle, surely!"

3. But it was, because it simply couldn't have been anything else. It was most peculiar, though. It had two wheels of a most extraordinary shape, and even queerer handle-bars!

4. "It must have fallen from a circus van," said John. "My goodness, isn't it dirty and muddy! Let's take it home and clean it, Jane, before we find out whose it is."

5. So the children took the strange bicycle home and spent a long time cleaning it. John tried to ride it but he at once fell off—and so did Jane! It really was difficult to ride!

6. They took it to the circus-field, shining bright—and a little man there came running up. "My bicycle!" he said. "Oh, I thought it was gone forever—it's all clean and shining too!"

7. Well, will you believe it, the peculiar bicycle belonged to the chief clown, and he was so pleased to have it back all clean and bright, that he gave the children two circus tickets...

8. And here they are at the circus—and how they clapped when they saw the chief clown come in, riding on the strange bicycle. And dear me, *he* kept falling off too!

They Did Like the Mud

"MUMMY, the swallows and the martins are back again!" cried Joan, running indoors to her mother. "They are flying about the sky just as they did last summer. I *am* glad they have come back, I was afraid they wouldn't."

"Oh, they always do," said Mummy. "Lovely things! I hope the house-martins will build their nests under the eaves of our house, Joan. You'd like that!"

"Mummy, I wish I could see them *closely*," said Joan. "They are always so high up in the sky, or they fly by me so quickly I can't see them. And I'd like to see the difference between the swallow and the martin properly. I wish I could make them come down into our garden."

"Well, you can," said Mummy. "It's dry weather just now, and I think you could bring the birds down here quite easily."

"But Mummy—however can I do that?" said Joan in surprise.

"Well, the swallows and martins like to have mud to build their nests," said Mummy. "And as it is dry weather now, and the puddles have all gone, and there is no pond very near here, the birds haven't any chance of getting mud unless they fly off to the river-bank, and that's a good way away. So, if you like to go down the garden, and pour some water on the earthy path by the rubbish-heap, I think maybe the martins and swallows will see it and fly down!"

Joan took her watering-can and ran down the garden. She made the path very muddy there and stirred it up a bit with a stick. Then she went inside the little shed, and watched quietly.

The martins saw the mud first. Down they swept and began to scoop it up in their tiny beaks! They chattered in little high voices, lovely to hear. Then the swallows came, and gathered up the mud too.

"Oh, you little dears!" said Joan, watching eagerly. "Now I know the difference between you! *You've* got a patch of white at the bottom part of your back, martins, and the swallows haven't. And *you* are a lovely steel-blue, swallows, with a patch of red on your throat and forehead! You've both got fine curving wings and forked tails!"

The happy birds scooped up the mud and flew off to make their nests. One pair of house-martins made a cup of mud just above Joan's bedroom window, under the eaves. She was so pleased. "Now I shall be able to see your baby birds when you have some," she said. "How clever you are at building a nest of beaks-ful of mud! *I* couldn't do that, I know."

The swallows built a saucer of mud for a nest, on a beam in the barn nearby. So Joan would be able to see the baby swallows too. She was very happy.

"I wish everybody knew how to bring the martins and swallows into their gardens!" she said. "They could easily do it if a dry spell came, couldn't they, Mummy? I wish somebody would tell all the children."

Well—I've told you. So see if you are lucky enough to bring them into *your* garden, too!

Benny's Robin

EVERYONE called the robin Benny's robin. It used to come and watch nearby when he was digging in his little garden in the autumn. When he turned up a grub, the robin would fly down and pick it up at once. Then it would carol a little song.

"That's your way of saying thank you," said Benny. "Dear little fellow —I'll give you crumbs in the winter, if you will come to the window."

So, in the winter, when there were no insects or grubs for the robin, the little bird learnt to look to Benny for food.

At breakfast-time each day it would fly right down to the window-sill, and peck at the pane, peck, peck, peck, peck-peck! Then Benny and his mother would hear it and smile.

"That's the robin, come for his breakfast," Benny would say. "I'll give him some crumbs."

Every day Benny opened the window and scattered crumbs on the window-sill. The robin pecked them up daintily. He never seemed greedy, like the sparrows or starlings. He would peck up a crumb, then sing a few notes, then peck up another crumb.

"He has very good manners," said Mother. "And isn't he tame, Benny!"

Benny was very fond of gardening, even in the winter. He always went to help the gardener when he came. He liked digging with him, planting seeds in the spring, and making a bonfire in the winter.

It was winter time now. The gardener had cut down all the old plants, and swept up the leaves, and was going to have a bonfire. Benny was longing to help him. "Will it go on burning all night?" he asked.

"No," said the gardener. "I'll put it out before I go. It's a bit too near the shed to leave burning all night. I'll light it again to-morrow."

"There's my little robin come to watch us," said Benny, as the robin flew down and stood on the handle of the gardener's fork. "Do you know where he sleeps at night, gardener? He sleeps in that shed!"

"Does he really?" said the gardener, putting old twigs on the blazing bonfire.

"Yes. I know because one night I took my torch and came out here to the shed to get something—and there, sleeping in an over-turned flower-pot, with its little head under its wing, was my robin!" said Benny.

"It's a real friend of yours," said the gardener, who liked robins too.

"Yes, it is. It comes and pecks on the window-pane for crumbs each morning, and sleeps in my shed at night!" said Benny. "The other day it pecked on the window at tea-time, because it was extra hungry in the cold!"

The gardener got the bonfire going well and then went off to do some digging. He left Benny in charge of it.

Benny liked looking after a bonfire. It was fun to fork rubbish on to it, and keep it going. He was sorry when tea-time came and the gardener said he must put it out.

"I'll light it again tomorrow," he promised, and forked big clods of earth on to it to smother it. "There—that's all right now. It's out. Good night, Benny."

Benny went in to tea. The robin flew into the shed through a broken pane, found his flower-pot and curled himself up there for the night, for it was getting dark already.

"I've had a lovely day, Mummy," said Benny, when he got into bed. "I smell all smoky still, though I've had a bath, or perhaps it's the clothes on my chair. I like the smell of the bonfire. I'm sorry it's out."

But it wasn't out! That night one little flame licked up from the middle of the bonfire and set a few dead leaves alight. Those set fire to some twigs—and soon the bonfire was burning merrily again. Crackle, crackle, crackle!

The wind got up in the night and blew the flames to the shed. The robin in the flower-pot pulled his head out from under his wing and wondered what

the bright light was outside the window. Then he felt a draught of hot air. He flew out of the pot and perched on the broken pane of the window. It was quite hot to his feet!

"Tirra-lee," said the robin to himself. "Tirra-lee! What is this happening in the middle of the night? It's something wrong, I am sure. Tirra-lee."

The robin felt that he would like to tell Benny. He flew off to the playroom window-sill. He tapped hard on the pane—peck, peck, peck. Peck, peck, peck.

But there was no one in the playroom, of course, because it was night-time. The robin didn't know that. He went on pecking harder and harder.

He made such a noise that Benny, asleep in his bedroom next to the playroom, heard it and awoke. He sat up. What was that noise? Tap-tap, tap-tap!

"How queer! It sounds like someone tapping at the playroom window," thought Benny, and he jumped out of bed. He ran into the playroom. Tap-tap, tap-tap!

Benny stopped. Through the window he could see the leaping flames of the bonfire out in the garden! By their light he could see the shape of the little robin outside the window.

"It was my robin pecking at the pane!" said Benny. Then he saw that the flames from the bonfire were licking against the wooden walls of the shed. He ran into his father's room.

"Mummy! Daddy! The bonfire is alight again and it's just going to burn the shed!"

His father leapt out of bed at once. He dragged on his coat and trousers, and then ran downstairs quickly. He rushed into the garden, and filled a pail of water. He threw it on the flames—sizzle-sizzle-sizzle!

Soon the fire was really out, and only black smoke rose up. Benny's father felt the side of the shed. It was hot. Another minute or two and the shed would have been on fire.

Benny was by his side, shivering in his dressing-gown. His father turned to him.

"Well, Benny, you saved our shed! Another few minutes and it would have been burnt and everything in it!"

"*I* didn't save it, Daddy," said Benny. "It was my robin. I heard him tapping hard on the window-pane, and when I went to see what the noise was, I saw the flames of the bonfire! My robin sleeps in the shed, you know—so he could see the bonfire blazing up again—and he came to tell me."

"Tirra-lee," said a little voice beside them, and there was the robin, perched on the sill of the shed-window.

"Thank you robin," said Benny. "You shall have a fine lot of crumbs to-morrow. You're a good friend!"

"Tirra-lee, you're a friend to me, tirro-loo, I'm a friend to you!" sang the robin, and hopped into the shed again. He was soon in his flower-pot, his head under his wing.

Benny still has his robin, who is tamer than ever. Have you a robin of your own, too? Well, go and work in the garden, and you will soon have one.

"Tirra-lee!" you will hear, and down will come a robin and look at you with big black eyes. "Tirra-lee!"

The Tale of the Tadpoles

THERE was once a small boy called Willie. He went fishing one day in a little pond where frogs had laid their eggs. They had laid them in jelly, but now, in the warm sunshine, the jelly had melted, and the eggs had hatched out into tiny black tadpoles.

How they wriggled and raced round the pond! They were queer little things, all tail and head—tailed-polls, or, as we say it for short, tadpoles.

Willie wondered what they were. He put some in a jar and took them home, with some pondweed for them to cling to if they wanted to.

"Look, Mother!" he said. "What are these? Haven't I got a lot of the little black wrigglers?"

"Yes, you have. Far too many," said his mother. "Now, Willie, you like frogs, don't you—well, these tiny wrigglers will all change into little frogs, if you take care of them properly. It will be like magic."

"Gracious! I'd like to watch them turning into frogs," said Willie, who couldn't imagine how they did it. "But have I really got too many, Mother? I'd like a *lot* of frogs, you know."

"Well, if you do what most children do, and keep dozens in a small jar, they will all die, for there will not be enough air in the water for them all to breathe," said his mother. "Take all but five or six of them back to the pond, Willie, and just keep those few."

So Willie kept five in his jam-jar, and watched them carefully. Mother showed him how to tie a tiny bit of meat on a string and hang it in the jar for them to nibble at. Then he pulled it out again so that it would not go bad, and make the water smelly and cloudy. He left the pondweed in because the tadpoles loved that.

One day he put them in the sun. The hot sun warmed the water, and soon the tadpoles rose to the top, turned over and looked as if they were dying. Willie rushed to his mother at once.

"Oh, *Willie*! They're slowly cooking in the sun, poor things!" said his mother, whipping them away to a cool corner, and putting a little cold water into the jar. "Poor creatures! I hope they won't die. Hundreds of poor

little tadpoles are cooked every year because children put them into the hot sun!"

"I didn't think," said Willie, sadly. "I do hope they'll be all right, Mother. I do like them so much."

They didn't die. They got better when they felt cool. So Willie was able to watch the magic that turned the tadpoles, all head and tail, into tiny frogs with four legs and a little squat body!

Their back legs grew, and then their front legs. Their tails became short. They didn't drop off, they simply grew short. Willie watched them each day, so he knew.

He gave them a cork to climb on, when they became tiny frogs, for now they liked to breathe the open air.

Then he put them into his garden to find new homes for themselves.

"Eat the grubs and flies for me," he said. "I've been a friend to you—now you be a friend to me!"

Would *you* like to see frog-magic too? Well, do as Willie did, and keep a few tadpoles in a jar.